IMAGES
of America

POINT PLEASANT

To John

[signature] April 21, 1995

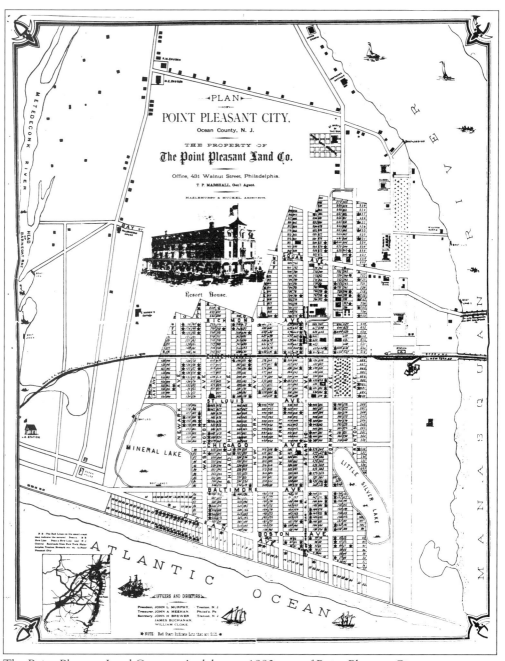

The Point Pleasant Land Company's elaborate 1880 map of Point Pleasant City.

IMAGES
of America

POINT PLEASANT

Compiled by
Jerry A. Woolley

ARCADIA

First published 1995
Copyright © Jerry A. Woolley, 1995

ISBN 0 7524 0096 7

Published by Arcadia Publishing,
an imprint of the Chalford Publishing Corporation,
One Washington Center, Dover, New Hampshire 03820.
Printed in Great Britain

Dedicated to my dear Grandmother Maude Holman Applegate Young,
for her love, guidance, and unending inspiration.

Contents

Of the dozens of real estate developments in the Point Pleasant area, Vesperland was one of the few that never got off the ground. Conceived in 1927 by Trenton promoters, the tract included all the land between Trenton and Arnold Avenues and from the railroad to the beach. Financial difficulties and tax liens kept the property untouched until after World War II.

Introduction

The history of the Point Pleasant area stretches back long before the era of photography to the earliest days of settlement in North America. This book picks up that long history with the invention of photography and carries it through to the recent recollections of many local people.

Point Pleasant and Point Pleasant Beach were once a part of Brick Township. Point Pleasant Beach became a separate borough in 1886, followed by Point Pleasant in 1920. An identity crisis plagued both towns for years, with the Beach referred to as "Point Pleasant" and the Boro as "West Point Pleasant." These were actually the names given to the post offices of the respective towns until the 1930s. In order not to confuse the reader, the name Point Pleasant refers to both towns as a whole while Point Pleasant Beach and Point Pleasant Borough refer to the individual communities.

While some of the photographs in this book may be familiar, most have never before been published. Many have been taken from the original glass plate negatives. The task of identifying people in these photographs is sometimes a difficult one. For example, the names of the schoolchildren on the cover (photographed at the first Point Pleasant Beach School in 1899), and of the group of boarders below (photographed at the Arverne House on Atlantic Avenue in 1898) have proven elusive and may be lost forever. Tracking down this kind of information is part of the challenge that makes the research of local history so satisfying.

I hope you enjoy traveling back through time with this book as much as I have enjoyed preserving and unlocking our local history.

Jerry A. Woolley
March 1995

Acknowledgments

I would especially like to thank my wife Lee, for her patience, love, and understanding while our house was turned into a research center during the production of this book. Grateful appreciation to those who have contributed in many different ways toward making this book possible, including: my parents, Stanley and Shirley Woolley for their recollections and support; my brother Scott Woolley; Tom Williams and Dick Strickler and the staff at the Ocean County Historical Society; the Ocean County Library and especially Barbara Kaden and Bob Jahn at the Point Pleasant Branch; the Point Pleasant Historical Society and its members for their support; Jay Newcomb for his photographic expertise; the staff at Hall Color Labs; Dotti Daly of the Greater Point Pleasant Area Chamber of Commerce; Russell Mickle of Point Pleasant Beach Fire Company No. 2; Chris Meyer of Shore Antique Center; John Walsh of Bay Pointe Engineering Associates; the late Arthur Johnson and his wife Jean; Antionette Downey Mayer; Emery Wheeler; Nancy Skinner; Jeff and Kathy Heim; Jim and Pat Malone; Betsy LeChard; Dick LaBonte; Dan DiCorcia; Alice Lane; Michael Loughran; Dr. Claribel Young; Betty Van Horn; and David Oxenford, who started the ball rolling for me in my senior year at Point Pleasant Beach High School.

One
The Seashore Resorts

The Resort House was the flagship of the Point Pleasant Land Company. It was the first of the large hotels that followed, and cost over $20,000. The four-story edifice was built in the spring of 1878 at the southwest corner of Richmond and Forman Avenues.

This boarding house was part of the Aumack Farm in the vicinity of Trenton and Arnold Avenues when it was sold to Charles W. Maxson and operated as a hotel and a public meeting house. Maxson was an early pioneer in the hotel trade, as well as a lifesaver, wreck master, and farmer. This hotel burned in 1880 and later became the site of Britton's Tavern and the Village Inn.

When Ebenezer Curtis first opened his farmhouse to Philadelphia boarders in the 1820s, little did he know the beautiful surroundings would become a magnet for some of the greatest literary and acting talents at the turn of the century. The main house (shown above) was located near the Manasquan River at what is today Orchard Avenue, and was surrounded by smaller cottages. The most famous of these, Vagabond's Rest, is all that remains of the Curtis Homestead.

The St. James Hotel was built in 1882 among the dunes between Arnold and Central Avenues. This view is looking west from the beach with the hotel bathing pavilion on the left. Mrs. A. Crawford ran the St. James for six seasons before tragedy struck in September of 1888, when fire consumed the hotel and killed a guest one day before the winter closing.

A group of guests from the Cook Homestead posed for this 1888 photograph in front of the St. James bathing pavilion and bath houses near the hotel at the foot of Arnold Avenue. The pavilion was a popular rendezvous for another four years before it was lost in a severe nor'easter (see page 53). Directly behind the pavilion ran Old Ocean Avenue, providing access for the hotel guests. The present boardwalk covers the original Ocean Avenue.

The Cook Homestead, dating from the Revolutionary War, opened its doors to summer guests about 1828 when Thomas Cook Jr. took over operation of the farm from his father. The main house stood just north of the present intersection of St. Louis Avenue and Niblick Street and survived 160 years before fire took its toll in 1942.

The members of the Cook family were Quakers, and their homestead was popular with Philadelphians. Most dancing, card playing, and spirits were not allowed; however, ample entertainment was provided on the 280-acre farm which ran from Parkway north to the Manasquan River and from the railroad east to the beach.

This 1895 view shows the road leading to the river from the Cook Homestead. The River and Oceanfront Land Improvement Company purchased the entire farm in 1902 for $62,000. They concentrated their efforts at the beach front, building a large pavilion and dance hall at the inlet the following year. In 1917, the Point Pleasant Golf Club built a 9-hole course on the tract and remodeled the homestead as a clubhouse and a tea room (see page 71).

One of the Cook barns serves as a backdrop for this 1895 gathering. Barns, stables, guest cottages, an ice house, and a pump house all helped to make the Cook Homestead and farm self-supporting. Two years after Thomas Cook died in 1874, William Reed and his family rented the farm and made many improvements over the following twenty years.

Captain John Arnold was the driving force behind the first real expansion of Point Pleasant into a resort community. After having spent his childhood in Point Pleasant and then twenty years as a sea captain, John Arnold returned to Point Pleasant and became a farmer. In 1868 the Arnold House was built and opened as a first-rate boarding house. To accommodate his guests, Captain Arnold constructed a roadway leading to the ocean, which is today Arnold Avenue. He was also instrumental in securing the first wagon bridge over the Manasquan River, established White Lawn Cemetery, and convinced the Central Railroad of New Jersey to extend its rail line south from Manasquan to Point Pleasant. The above view shows the Arnold House in 1878. The road in the foreground is Arnold Avenue near the present Europa South Restaurant; the view is looking north.

Captain John Arnold was born in 1818 to John and Ann (Williams) Arnold. His father, an English Quaker, died prior to his birth and his mother brought him to Point Pleasant in 1820. John Arnold died in November of 1886, at the height of his popularity.

The Arnold House, later named the Maple Grove Hotel, continued to operate into the 1920s. In 1926 a new three-story hotel was built on the site complete with twenty-three rooms and a restaurant (below). The Hotel Arnold continued as an important establishment in Point Pleasant Beach until fire gutted the top two floors in March 1956. It was rebuilt as a one-story bar/restaurant. Another fire in 1961 ended ninety-three years of a landmark business.

The Point Pleasant Land Company's Resort House on Richmond Avenue between Forman and Atlantic Avenues in 1895. New owners doubled the size of the hotel that year, providing 109 sleeping rooms, a large dining room, ball room, reception room, billiard room, and office. Steam heat, electric lights, indoor lavatories, and an elevator were also added. After falling on hard times, the hotel was renamed the Warwick Arms in 1902 and burned to the ground in December 1909.

A view of Point Pleasant City on August 30, 1884, from atop the Resort House bathing pavilion at the foot of Atlantic Avenue. The horse-drawn trolley took hotel guests to and from the beach between 1878 and 1890. The cross street near the center of the photograph is Baltimore Avenue. Notice the lack of vegetation, as the tract was still in a transition from farms to developed properties. The original Forman Farm was started after the Revolutionary War by Samuel Forman, whose son took over the farm in the early 1800s. John S. Forman began taking boarders in the 1820s and gradually built a solid reputation for his homestead as a first-rate destination for city dwellers escaping the summer heat. Forman also served as wreck master and county judge, and before his death turned over the operation to his son Sidney, who in turn sold the 250-acre farm and homestead to the Point Pleasant Land Company in 1877. The Forman Homestead was located on what is today the northwest corner of Forman and Richmond Avenues, and among its many attractions was the first bowling alley in town. An annex was located to the rear, which still exists today at 607 Forman Avenue.

Opposite, bottom: The Tower Cottage was among the first dozen houses built in Point Pleasant City in the early 1880s. At this time lots along the oceanfront were being offered for $2,500 while the Tower Cottage lot on Little Silver Lake sold for $600. This house still stands, minus the tower, at 203 Forman Avenue.

B.L. Garrison's West Point Pleasant Hotel *c.* 1895. This hotel was built by Charles W. Maxson in 1870 and was known as Maxson's Point Pleasant Hotel. Among the sporting events featured here were clay pigeon shooting and turkey hunts. The building ceased operation as a hotel by the late 1940s and today is the Fireside Inn at Route 88 and Herbertsville Road.

The Lands End Hotel was a fixture at New Jersey and Boston Avenues for eighty years. Built by the Point Pleasant Land Company in 1883 and complimented by two connected cottages across the street, this hotel outlasted all but one of Point Pleasant's original hotels. The Lands End Cottages still stand at 100 and 102 New Jersey Avenue.

The Hotel Marion was built in 1893 by Lawrence Vannote as the town's first year-round hotel. The hotel was named after Vannote's son. The building was later owned by world cycle champion Arthur Zimmerman and from 1928 to 1933 contained the Borough Hall and lockup. After one hundred years the building, now known as the Valentine House at 605 Bay Avenue, still houses guests.

Built in 1899, the Pine Bluff Inn was located on the Manasquan River just east of the present canal entrance. Originally operated as a temperance house, the hotel was surrounded by a grove of pines and was a popular alternative to the beach front hotels. A 6-hole golf course, tennis court, dance floor, and sailing on the river were among the Pine Bluff Inn's many attractions. The hotel was closed during the Great Depression and was torn down in the early 1940s.

The Ocean House was built about 1860 at the foot of what is today Sea Avenue. It started out as more a gathering place for Barnegat Bay gunners than a hotel, but by the 1870s it gained popularity as a summer hotel on the beach. A mineral spring was discovered near the hotel in 1877 which prompted proprietor Charles Sutterly to promote the Ocean House as a first-class health resort.

The Ocean House was renamed Beacon-By-The-Sea in 1893 and continued its popularity with the addition of tennis courts, a 9-hole golf course, and a bathing pavilion (see page 115). These attractions came and went with the times and the hotel itself was eventually absorbed into the Beacon Manor Motel/Restaurant complex in the early 1960s. The last remaining traces of a hotel on the site ended in 1994 when the Oceanside Sheraton was demolished.

Point Pleasant's largest hotel, the Hotel Leighton, was built in 1893 on the dunes between Trenton and Forman Avenues. It originally contained seventy-seven rooms but was later enlarged to ninety-one rooms, including a huge kitchen and ballroom. The Leighton tennis courts were adjacent to the hotel and were the site of many national tournaments. The east end of the hotel was destroyed in a storm in 1929 (see page 117) and the Leighton was finally dismantled in 1943.

The Carrollton Hotel was located on the northwest corner of Atlantic and Boston Avenues. It was built in 1898 by John A. Casey of Brooklyn, who named the hotel after his friend and summer resident, J.W. Carroll. After a very successful first season, the Carrollton was enlarged. A ballroom, cafe, and telegraph office were also featured. The Carrollton was destroyed in a spectacular fire on May 1, 1930.

James Dorsett purchased land in the southeast part of Point Pleasant Borough prior to 1800 and built the Dorsett Homestead, shown *c.* 1895. Dorsett's son John B. and grandson John Lott Dorsett farmed the land, as well as creating an important ship building business on Beaver Dam Creek. The homestead was located near the creek, east of Dorsett Dock Road, and survived into the late 1930s.

Captain John L. Dorsett with his grandson standing next to the figurehead of the Duke of Argyle, which he salvaged from the wreck of the barque *Argyle* in 1851. Dorsett was appointed keeper of Life Saving Station #9 in 1862; later he moved to Station #11 until his retirement from the service in 1876.

After retiring from the Life Saving Service, Dorsett built and sailed some of the finest yachts on Barnegat Bay. The *Rosemond* was his last large pleasure yacht and served as the flagship of the Island Heights Yacht Club for several years. The *Rosemond* was a familiar sight on the bay and is shown here in 1900. After Dorsett's death in 1910, the *Rosemond* was abandoned on Beaver Dam Creek.

Dorsett's son John A. continued his father's boat building concern, shown above with his finest achievement, the 45-foot cabin cruiser *Mon Desire*, built for J. Luther Bright of Elberon. Retiring from sailing and boat building in 1930, Dorsett and his wife concentrated on their already thriving sail making business (see page 45). John A. Dorsett was also a surveyor and served as assessor of Brick Township and Point Pleasant Borough.

COTILLION PARTY

AT

D. W. White's Hotel,

POINT PLEASANT.

Mr Lawrence Denver & Lady

The pleasure of your company is respectfully
solicited to attend a Cotillion
Party at

Daniel W. White's Hotel,

Point Pleasant,

Thursday Evening, Dec. 10th, 1857,

AT HALF PAST SEVEN O'CLOCK.

COMMITTEE.

A. A. HIGGINS,	SIDNEY HERBERT,
CHARLES MAXSON,	HENRY MOUNT,
WM. CRAIG,	JOHN M. ALLEN,
JACKSON DAVIDSON.	

Daniel White's Hotel was a very early inn and tavern located near Herbertsville and Lakewood Roads. Known earlier as Wainwright's Tavern, the hotel burned prior to 1870.

Two

Business As It Was

The Point Pleasant Lumber Company had already been in business for four years when James M. VanNote and William Errickson purchased the firm in 1885 and built it into a thriving lumber yard. When Errickson left the partnership in 1894, VanNote renamed the firm J.M. VanNote Lumber and moved the lumber sheds and office north across Arnold Avenue to his own property and its present location. The original office is shown here in the late 1890s.

The Ocean County Coal and Ice Company was established in 1906 by Harry and Edward Wardell on Hawthorne Avenue, on what is today the site of Point Bay Fuel. Posing in this 1911 photograph are, from left to right: Edna Havens, Billy Rilley, Harry Wardell, Harold Christie, Edward Wardell, Freeman Smith, Harry Vannote, a young Harry Stokes, William J. Stokes, Warren Britton, Sam Maxson, and Sox, the Irish setter.

The brand new B.F. Coles Real Estate office and dwelling on Railroad Square in 1895. The brick building to the right would later become the first home of the Ocean County National Bank. The Coles Building burned in the big Havens fire in 1903.

The intersection of Arnold and Richmond Avenues *c.* 1910 showing the Richmond Hotel and Bissey's Tavern, which was run by H.W. and J.R. Bissey. The thirteen-room hotel was built in 1903 and the barroom was opened in 1905. When the Bissey family sold the business in 1967, the new owners restored the building to near its original look and the establishment still operates today as Europa South Restaurant.

The Hotel Richmond bar *c.* 1910, featuring peanuts on the bar, nickel beers, and quarter lunches. Hand-painted roses decorate the walls. Prohibition closed the bar in 1918 and it was remodeled into a delicatessen and later a sporting goods store. The bar re-opened with the repeal of prohibition in 1933.

This busy scene shows an unpaved Arnold Avenue looking west from Cincinnati Avenue in the spring of 1895. The large structure on the right was the J.G.W. Havens Building, built the previous year. Havens, who was a state senator and superintendent of the Life Saving Service in New Jersey, kept his office here. The building also housed a bicycle shop, grocery, the *Beacon* newspaper, and several offices.

Frank Chamberlain's bicycle shop on Arnold Avenue in the Havens Building *c.* 1898. Frank was married to Ida Reed Chamberlain, whose family ran the Cook Farm in the latter part of the nineteenth century (see page 13). Chamberlain lost his business when the Havens Building burned to the ground in August 1903.

Arnold Avenue looking west from the railroad after the big snowstorm of March 1914. The building on the extreme left was the Knox Building, the first home of Point Pleasant Hardware Company. On the right is Ocean County National Bank when the main entrance was to the east on Railroad Square.

The Ocean County National Bank was established March 18, 1901, and quickly became one of the largest banking institutions in the county. After the Havens fire, the bank secured the corner lot and built the familiar stone and brick building that still stands today, much enlarged and now owned by Summit Bank. Shown above is the first expansion in 1923 which included moving the main entrance to Arnold Avenue, and the addition of a new vault (right).

The Point Pleasant Hardware Company was established in 1885 by Joseph Backes and Charles Cline in the Knox Building on Arnold Avenue. In 1890, the business was sold to Philadelphians Joseph Johnson and Frank Dampman. The latter was bought out in 1892, and Johnson built the store into the most successful hardware business in Ocean County, which continued under his son and grandson until it was closed in 1990. New owner Robert Wehner re-opened the business in 1991 as a ServicStar hardware. The store in the above 1910 photograph was built in 1902.

George P. Buckelew (right) was already a successful businessman in Farmingdale when he opened his Point Pleasant butcher shop with his son William (left) in the Laug Building on Arnold Avenue about 1908. Buckelew's also kept a large stock of groceries and canned goods on hand.

When O.B. Van Camp closed his grocery business in the Goodman Building and went into real estate, Buckelew's Market moved into the vacant store in 1910 and remained there for nearly forty years. The store's interior is shown above with George Buckelew (left), son William (right), and Dave Fleming (second from the right), *c.* 1920.

Buckelew's later became franchised with the Royal Scarlet Stores chain. This May 1943 photograph shows a fresh delivery of milk, the old fashioned way. After Buckelew's closed, Winograd's Department Store took over the site, adding a new facade and becoming an important downtown business leader. The Goodman Building, originally built about 1891, and an adjoining building were demolished in 1988.

This building on the southeast corner of Bay and Arnold Avenues had an interesting history. Built as a general store in 1879 by John Arnold and expanded to the south and east in the early 1880s, the Arnold Building became the center of commerce in the growing community. In this 1893 photograph the establishment consisted of the Eureka Boarding House, Headley and Van Camp Groceries and Provisions, the post office, and apartments above.

If you stood on Arnold Avenue in 1898 and looked south down Bay Avenue, this is what you would see. The Albert Allen property is on the right. In the distance can be seen the three-story Hendrickson and Huss Buildings. The trolley tracks can be faintly seen running down the center of Bay Avenue (see page 60).

Gottlieb's Point Pleasant Department Store opened in the Arnold Building in 1898 and is shown here in 1904. John Henry ran the grocery store to the left. The Gottlieb family lived in the apartment above their store which was rented from Guelma Johnson, who owned the building at this time. The Eureka Boarding House was at this point the Central House, run by Mrs. Fred Wood and catering mostly to railroad workers.

The Gottlieb Department Store in the Johnson Building shortly before the devastating fire of 1906. Michael Gottlieb purchased a lot across Arnold Avenue next to John Arnold Hall in the winter of 1906 and planned to build a new store and apartments the following summer. It is as if he foresaw the firestorm that was to come.

In the early morning hours of March 21, 1906, Point Pleasant's business center was consumed in fire. Eight businesses were lost as well as the post office and the William Todd residence. The aftermath is shown above, with Makin's Bakery and Arnold Hall (center) surviving with minor damage. The Ocean Fire Company was headquartered in Arnold Hall at this time.

This photograph was taken from Arnold Hall with Arnold Avenue in the foreground. The inferno was stopped at E.T. Van Camp's restaurant on Bay Avenue and at the Clickener House on Arnold Avenue. The Gottliebs barely escaped the fire: after climbing out of their apartment windows in their nightclothes, they were carried to safety by the volunteers of Ocean Fire Company.

Michael Gottlieb's new department store on Arnold Avenue in 1912. The post office occupied the storefront to the left between 1906 and 1917. The Gottlieb family can be seen standing at the entrance to the store. Gottlieb's Department Store remained in business for over eighty years.

John Arnold Hall, shown here in 1910, was an important community center. Ocean Fire Company No. 1, Johnson's Pharmacy, and the Borough Council chambers occupied the first floor. The town hall, complete with a stage, dressing rooms, and seating for 250 filled the second floor, while the third floor contained a lodge room and banquet facilities. The Ocean Fire Company erected Arnold Hall in 1899 and it still exists today, minus the third floor.

A view of Clinton W. Coles Dry Goods and Groceries on Bay Avenue in 1895. Benjamin Coles began the business about 1890 and sold out to his son and Clarence Lippincott. A fire in 1899 destroyed this building and another store adjacent to the south. Bay Point Optical occupies the site today.

Fred and William Makin's Point Pleasant Bakery at Arnold and Bay Avenues c. 1915. This very popular bakery was started by Stephen Henry Pearce in 1893 and was sold to Fred Makin in 1903. A bakery continued to be conducted on the site until the building was damaged by fire in 1932 and torn down. Shown here are William H. Makin, daughter Mary, son William Jr., and employee Alfred Pearce.

The newly rebuilt Laug Building is shown in this wonderful photograph taken in 1907. Councilman and candy maker John Laug began his business in the mid-1890s and lost everything in the 1906 fire. He rebuilt his candy factory to near its original appearance and continued for several more years before pursuing business interests in Lakewood.

Laug's delivery truck at the rear of his store c. 1910. Laug manufactured his own ice cream and fountain soda flavors, which were the ultimate prize of any child who could manage to save 5¢ for a Laug Ice Cream soda.

Zebulon P. VanNote's Livery and Boarding Stables on Bay Avenue in 1895. VanNote began his livery in a barn at his home on Forman Avenue in 1883 and moved it to the Bay Avenue site in 1886. Excursion stages, roundabouts, buckboards, phaetons, and victorias were all available for hire with or without drivers. VanNote's Stables met its demise at the hand of the automobile around 1930 when Zeb VanNote retired at the age of seventy-two.

Clayton's Feed Store at 612 Bay Avenue in the Hendrickson Building c. 1918. From left to right are: Eldore, Freddie, and Ross. Several feed stores operated on Bay Avenue in the early 1900s. The largest was Point Pleasant Supply Company which was at Bay and Laurel Avenues.

A bustling Arnold Avenue looking east from Bay Avenue in 1928. Arnold Avenue was a gravel main street until 1924 when concrete pavement was laid. Concrete was also poured on Bay, Richmond, Forman, and Ocean Avenues in 1924. Next to Lakewood, Point Pleasant Beach had the largest amount of concrete paving in Ocean County.

The Grove Theater was built by Ralph Borden and Alonzo Carver in 1920 on Arnold Avenue. This 1925 photograph shows the theater and the recently opened Borden's United Cigar Store on the right, which was the predecessor of the modern Borden's. The Grove closed after being damaged by fire in 1950, but the building still exists today at 607 and 609 Arnold Avenue behind a modern facade.

After spending nine years under the employ of butchers George and William Buckelew, Fred Pearce opened his own meat store with his brother Robert at 518 Bay Avenue in 1918. Fred Pearce is shown here outside his store in 1921. This building was torn down for a parking lot in 1968.

The Griggs Building on the corner of Arnold and River Avenues in 1923. J.W. Lawrence Hardware and Bailey's Novelty Store occupied the two storefronts. The building, which still stands, was built in 1917 by Edward Griggs, who operated an ice cream stand on the corner and lived in the apartment above with his family.

Point Pleasant had its share of Chinese laundries in their heyday. One of the earliest was a laundry and notions store in 1892. The Rising Sun Chinese Laundry on Bay Avenue is shown above in June 1945.

Sally's Curb Service at Richmond Avenue and Ocean Road in April 1933. Sally's was a chain of restaurants in the state that featured outdoor barbecue pits and lighted picnic areas. Sally's came and went, but the building remained under various owners until the dualization of Route 35 in 1966.

The Huss/Height and Lawrence Building at Bay and Trenton Avenues in 1895. Bay Head builder Wyckoff Applegate built the store and apartments for butcher John Huss in 1893. Huss ran a successful meat market until 1902, when the concern was sold to Height and Lawrence, and it was continued as a butcher shop until about 1930. The building still stands, minus the third floor which burned off in 1944.

Bay Avenue, as seen from Johnson's Furniture Mart at Bay and Trenton Avenues c. 1954. McLaughlin's Toy Store is on the right in the old Huss Building. The building on the left served as the original Borough Hall from 1886 to 1893. Next is VanNote's Stables, now VanCulin's Chrysler Auto Dealer. Both of these buildings burned in a spectacular fire in 1961.

42

Charles Van Schoick was working for Sheffield Farms when he decided to go into business for himself and start his own dairy. Van Schoick's Pleasant Farms Dairy was established in 1937 at Richmond and Philadelphia Avenues and continued to operate until 1964. The building was expanded with a retail store in the early 1950s and is shown above in 1958.

Makin Manufacturing Company at Washington and Cincinnati Avenues in 1960. Started in 1932 by William and George Makin, concrete blocks were made by hand-operated machinery at the rate of 250 blocks a day. The company gradually expanded to include a full line of mason material and the manufacturing of bricks. The business moved to the east side of the railroad after the construction of Route 35 North in 1966 and today the WaWa strip mall is on the site.

Tommy Haven's General Store *c.* 1910. Many establishments of this type existed in the area during this period. Haven's store was on the south side of Lakewood Road midway between Arnold Avenue and the present Point Pleasant Canal. West Point Pleasant's center of commerce was located here and at Herbertsville Road, dating back to the 1840s.

Another small business center was situated at Arnold and Trenton Avenues in West Point Pleasant. Hance's Hall was a three-story building that housed lodge rooms and a meeting hall on the upper floors and C.V. Hance's General Store on the street level. The hall was built in 1895 on the southwest corner of the intersection and burned in 1910. Charles Hance is shown above outside his store in 1899. Alfred Holman, mayor of Point Pleasant Borough in 1933–34, is outside his barber shop enjoying the summer weather.

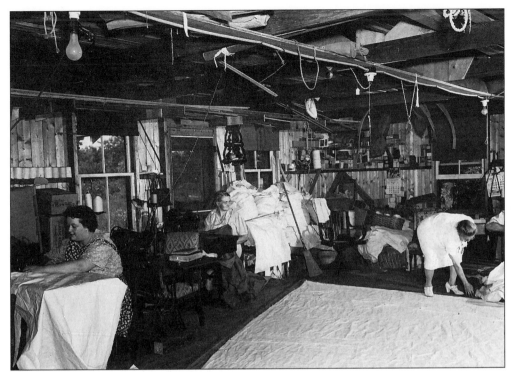

The busy interior of Dorsett's Sail Shop at Dorsett Dock Road and Bridge Avenue in June 1942. After John A. Dorsett's death, Mrs. Dorsett continued the business through the 1940s. Mrs. Dorsett is spreading a sail on the floor (right) while Mrs. John Jamison sews the sail sections together (left).

While Point Pleasant Beach enjoyed the benefit of a municipal sewer system back to the turn of the century, Point Pleasant Borough residents utilized underground septic tanks until the 1970s. Falkinburg Sanitary Engineer provided longtime septic service to Point Pleasant and Brick Township. One of Falkinburg's earlier trucks is shown here in June 1943.

Joseph Metzler's Garage on Lakewood Road in Point Pleasant Borough in November 1941. Located on the corner of Oakwood Road, the building continued as an auto garage until the front half was removed for the new Route 88 canal bridge project in the early 1980s.

The Stanwall Inn was a popular tavern on Lakewood Road at the corner of Central Avenue. The bar and restaurant was later expanded into the parking lot, shown here in October 1945. Like Metzler's, the Stanwall was demolished when the property was acquired for the canal bridge project.

R.H. LeChard and Sons Marine Contractors had a long-time association with waterfront construction in Point Pleasant. LeChard was involved during and after the construction of the Manasquan-Bay Head Canal. Here, a LeChard dredge is moored in the canal in 1943.

Service stations sprang up like mushrooms in Point Pleasant during the 1920s and 30s. An early example was James Jaehnel's Esso Station on Lakewood Road and Curtis Avenue in June 1938. Jaehnel also rented cabins, later selling both businesses to A. Wenke, who built Wenke's Motel on the site of the service station.

By 1917 the Point Pleasant Beach Post Office had outgrown the cramped quarters in the Gottlieb Building (see page 35) and moved into a new facility, shown here at 518 Arnold Avenue. The land and building were donated to the town by newspaper magnate Arthur Brisbane, who owned considerable land in Point Pleasant. The post office moved to its present location in 1958.

John Arnold Hall at Arnold and River Avenues after the blizzard of March 1914. This was one of the worst snowstorms to ever hit the shore with over 2 feet of snow and 60 mph winds. Train service was suspended and the town went without electricity for two days. This was what we call today an old fashioned winter!

The Custom Auto Store was located at 522 Arnold Avenue in the old Downey Building. Henry Downey of Osbornville built this building in 1894 at the corner of Arnold and Richmond Avenues. It was moved east one lot when Johnson's Point Pleasant Hardware Store was built in 1902 and was eventually torn down when the hardware store expanded in 1960. The above photograph was taken in March 1947.

A view of, from left to right: Grove Theater, Borden's, and the Arnold Hotel, c. 1938. Ralph Borden opened his United Cigar Store on Richmond Avenue to the rear of the present Borden's in 1918, and with his son William, moved the store into the Grove Theater in 1925. The present store was built in 1930 and expanded to the corner in 1935. Liquor, firearms, and ammunition were featured items at Borden's in the 1920s and 30s.

The southwest corner of Bridge Avenue and Beaver Dam Road in June 1950. One of the earliest stores in this future business district was Hood's Market and Deli which later became Spader's Market and today houses Vesuvio Pizza. The future home of Hennessy's Service Station can be seen under construction on the corner.

John's Restaurant was one of the early restaurants to open on Broadway. The first location, shown here in 1945, is today the home of Portofino Restaurant. John's then moved to a new location on Broadway, and eventually became Rudy's and the Italian Fisherman, which burned in 1982.

The Point Pleasant Motor Company at Bay and Trenton Avenues in May 1943. The Ford dealership was started in 1921 on the site of the former Warren VanNote stables, and was operated by Howard Height of Manasquan until 1945 when it was sold to Roy and William Basso and Tally Pasino. Pasino went on to establish Tally's Dodge on Bridge Avenue, while the Basso brothers continued to run the garage and an Oldsmobile dealership until 1983.

Jack Curtis and Joe Makin started the Ship Chandlers store in the mid-1930s at 515 Bay Avenue. In 1949 the store moved to its present location. The business, shown above in July 1937, specialized in marine hardware and fishing tackle. The Ship Chandlers first home was in the Hochberg Building, built in 1900, which today houses Everybody's General Store.

GROVE THEATRE

POINT PLEASANT

1 Day Only—TUESDAY, JULY 31st—1 Day Only

SPECIAL PRE-RELEASE SHOWING OF

DAWN

with SYBIL THORNDIKE as NURSE CAVELL

This is the picture that has brought international acclaim! 'Dawn' outranks any picture yet produced in emotional tenseness! It is hailed by the press, pulpit and the public as the most human document ever presented on any screen.

Matinee 3 P. M.—20c and 30c   Evening—30c and 50c

The Grove on Arnold Avenue was probably the most popular of many theaters to be operated in Point Pleasant. Others included the Arnold Theater, the Riviera on Bay Avenue (now the Golden Eagle Restaurant), the Empire on Bay Avenue opposite the Riviera, the Gem open air theater next to the Empire, and several other open air movie houses in town and at the beach pavilions.

Three

The Journey To ...

The end of Arnold Avenue at the beach in 1890. On the left is the St. James Pavilion and bathhouses (see page 11). The impressive structure on the right was known as King's Pavilion and bathhouses and featured a three-story lookout tower. Both structures were lost in a violent coastal storm in March 1892.

This quiet, shady street is River Avenue at its intersection with Arnold Avenue in 1905. Arnold Hall is on the left. Until the advent of concrete paving in 1923, the main thoroughfares were topped with gravel and soil. The secondary roads were packed with soil or occasionally just sand in the remote areas.

Looking west on Arnold Avenue from River Avenue, after the snowstorm of 1914 (see page 48). The residence on the left was owned by William Todd, who ran a bottling establishment and later a process stone manufacturing company on Herbertsville Road near the present St. Martha's Church. The Todd House was moved to the rear when Todd built the present building at 636 Arnold Avenue in 1916 (today it is the Provident Bank).

This view of Arnold Avenue was taken in July 1948. The chamber of commerce had just succeeded in having parking meters installed on Arnold, Bay, and Richmond Avenues. The meters were removed in 1994.

Compare this view of Arnold Avenue thirty-four years later to the one on the left. In the above photograph, the Abromowitz Department Store at Bay and Arnold Avenues can be seen on the left. David Abromowitz opened his business in the cement Wheeler Building on the far left in 1910, and built his own store in 1924. The Abromowitz Department Store was a leading retailer in Point Pleasant until it closed its doors in 1978.

Sea Avenue looking west at the railroad crossing in September 1930. Notice the flagman's shanty to the left. Sea Avenue has been known by several names, such as the Road to the Sea, Road to Johnson's Hotel (Beacon Hotel), and Cod Fish Row. Today it is a part of Route 35.

Ocean Road was once loosely called Sea Captain Row for the abundance of active and retired sea salts who lived there. This view is of Ocean Road, looking west toward the intersection with Bay Avenue, in 1924. The Whittley House (center) stood near where a 7 Eleven is located today.

The Point Pleasant Parkway near Boston Avenue in July 1944. The parkway was cut through in 1920 by the J. Edward Ellor Corporation, which had purchased the property north of Central Avenue known as the old Curtis Tract. The first four houses on the street were built by the Ellors in 1920 on the four corners at Baltimore Avenue.

These two houses still exist, but not where they were when this photograph was taken in 1925. This was the intersection of Cincinnati and Forman Avenues at the rail crossing. The water company standpipe is in the background. The two homes were moved to Arbutus Avenue in 1958 when St. Peters School purchased the site for their new gymnasium, which was built in 1962.

Visitors to Point Pleasant Beach traveling south over the Manasquan River bridge in May 1941 were greeted by a welcome sign, flag pole, and World War I cannon at Richmond and River Avenues. The captured German cannon was dedicated on July 6, 1925, as a monument to veterans of World War I. A bronze tablet contained the names of 170 veterans. The cannon rests today at Little Silver Lake.

The intersection of Lakewood Road (Route 88) and Herbertsville Road in August 1948. West Point Pleasant Tavern is on the far left. This important intersection was the center of commerce in Point Pleasant during the early and mid-1800s. Herbertsville Road dates back to 1822 and was also known as Burnt Tavern Road. This name still applies today to the extension of Herbertsville Road east of the canal.

A view of Herbertsville Road, looking east toward Lakewood Road and the canal in 1948. One of Point Pleasant Borough's oldest garages was the Colonial (right). Ely's Diner is in the distance, which was later the site of the Waterway Motel. All of the buildings in this photograph, as well as the intersection, have since disappeared.

Eastbound on Lakewood Road near Metzler's Garage (right) in November 1941. Lakewood Road dates back to the early 1800s and was known as the Road to Burrsville or the Road to Point Pleasant, depending on which end you were at. This road became the first "improved" road built by Ocean County in 1903.

In this 1915 photograph the electric trolley line was in its twenty-first season. At the time of this picture, power for the cars came from Lakewood courtesy the Lakewood and Coast Electric Company, the trolley power house on Atlantic Avenue having been decommissioned the previous year. This trolley car is heading west on Arnold Avenue from its stop at the railroad station.

The South Jersey Street Railway Company began trolley service in Point Pleasant Beach on August 2, 1894. The line ran from the railroad station west on Arnold Avenue to Bay Avenue where it turned south on Bay and went as far as Atlantic Avenue. Here it turned east on Atlantic and ran to the beach. In 1895 the line was extended south to the Beacon Hotel and west on Arnold Avenue to Clarks Landing. In this photograph, one of the five cars that operated is shown on Atlantic Avenue *c.* 1910.

This unusual view of a trolley heading west on Arnold Avenue was taken from Arnold Hall *c.* 1912. The Laug Building at Arnold and River Avenues is in the background. The Street Railway Company was sold in 1896 and became the Bay Head and Point Pleasant Street Railway Company. A sheriff sale in 1902 again resulted in new owners and a new name: the Point Pleasant Traction Company.

The trolley line was finally extended into Bay Head in June 1903 and is shown above at its southern terminus on Lake Avenue *c.* 1912. By 1916 the tracks were also run into West Point Pleasant, bringing service to the Pine Bluff Inn. The Point Pleasant Traction Company ran its last car on the line in September 1919.

After a dozen years of requests and petitions, the railroad came to Point Pleasant in 1880, with the first passenger train arriving on July 3. The original station, shown above in 1888, served the community for twenty-two years before it was replaced. It was located west of the tracks near Arnold Avenue, where Route 35 North is today.

The municipal parking lot east of the tracks once was the site of the railroad yards, complete with ice house, water tanks, and turntable. The original roundhouse burned in 1898. The second one is shown here *c.* 1908 with the engine house crew. Yard master Ralph Bruno is fourth from the right.

In 1918 the loop at Bay Head Junction was put in service and started the demise of the Point Pleasant yard. Camelback steam engines such as the one above in 1917 were a common sight on the New York and Long Branch. The last Camelback ran on this line on July 11, 1954. The old Point Pleasant rail yard was closed on October 4, 1930, ending fifty years of service.

A stone station with slate roof and chestnut pillars replaced the original depot in 1903. This station, shown here serving a large Fourth of July crowd in 1943, lasted for sixty-three years before it was demolished during the dualization of Route 35 in 1966.

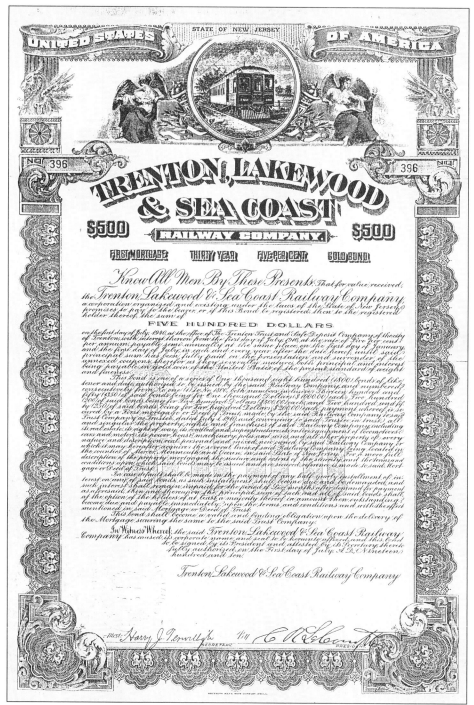

In 1915 stock was issued in the Trenton, Lakewood, and Seacoast Railway Company, a never completed railway between Trenton and Point Pleasant dating back to 1903. Track was actually laid on the line's eastern end between the Pine Bluff Inn and the present Point Pleasant-Brick Township border. However, trouble plagued the project at every turn and the corporation folded in 1923.

Four
Recreation and Education

The Point Pleasant Library Association first opened a free circulating library in Borough Hall in July 1894. In 1896 the library building was built on McLean Avenue on land given by William Curtis and with a donation of $500 by Emily Wood. The library, shown above in 1958, is now a part of the Ocean County Library System but still retains much of its early charm.

The Mid-Summer Frolic on Arnold Avenue in 1927. This four-day event was started in 1923 to benefit the Paul Kimball Hospital in Lakewood and was held during the second week of August. Featured events included the crowning of Queen Iris as well as a huge baby parade, block parties, and water sports at Clarks Landing. The Mid-Summer Frolic gained in popularity each year through the 1920s before falling victim to the Great Depression in 1931.

The baby parade often took center stage at the Mid-Summer Frolic and featured creative costumes and floats. A grandstand and judging platform were set up in Brisbane Park on Arnold Avenue, opposite the Grove Theater. In 1929, the grandstand was moved to Richmond Avenue where Food Town is today.

The Mid-Summer Frolic Baby Parade was said to rival Asbury Park's and was attended for several years by New Jersey Governors Moore and Larson.

Another featured float and contestant in the Mid-Summer Frolic Baby Parade in Point Pleasant Beach. All of these photographs were taken from glass plate negatives shot in 1928.

Big Sea Day on Manasquan Beach in 1896. Big Sea Day began as a custom of the early settlers and farmers, who would come to the shore on the second Saturday in August. Big Sea Day died with the coming of the automobile, but in 1913 was revived for several years along the Manasquan River in Point Pleasant.

Big Sea Day was again resurrected in 1950 in conjunction with Ocean County's centennial celebration. This time the event was sponsored by the Greater Point Pleasant Chamber of Commerce and enjoyed runaway success through the 1950s. Here, the Abromowitz Department Store float is shown heading down Arnold Avenue in the 1955 Big Sea Day Parade.

The Miss Seafood beauty contest was among the main events of the Ocean County Big Sea Days in Point Pleasant Beach. In this photograph Joan Mehok of Elberon is shown being chosen queen at the high school auditorium in 1955.

In 1961 Big Sea Day was held in conjunction with Point Pleasant Beach's diamond anniversary. Organizers of the celebration were, from left to right: (front) Robert Clark, Dr. C. Norman Witte, Dr. Eugene Roszko, Jess Pearce, Mrs. Helen Rogers, Mrs. Elsie Kolman, Mrs. Doris Cherry, and Mrs. Jean Yates; (back) Robert Connolly, Harold Benz, Lucien D. Truhill, and George Brown. The junior chamber of commerce took over Big Sea Day in 1962 and it continued on a smaller scale for two more years.

The Mohawk Athletic Clubhouse was located on the north side of Trenton Avenue just west of Cramer Avenue. The clubhouse was opened in 1903 and contained reception and reading rooms in the front and a large assembly hall housing the largest indoor basketball court in South Jersey at that time.

The Mohawk Athletic Club was formed in November 1901 "for the promotion of athletic amusements." Members of the club basketball team c. 1910 were, from left to right: (front row) Dorie Pearce and Ralph Borden; (middle row) Preston VanNote and Walter Makin; (back row) Henry Graham, manager Lon Carver, and Yetman Pearce.

A local football team was formed in Point Pleasant in the mid-1890s to compete against similar teams in the shore area. On the steps of the Marion Hotel is the 1893 football squad, which evolved into a highly competitive team over the following two years. After a hard win by Manasquan over Point in 1894, the Squan papers dubbed the Point players as "sluggers." It must have been some game!

Golf had always been a popular pastime for residents and visitors to Point Pleasant. The Point Pleasant Golf Club was organized in the early 1900s and built golf links at the Pine Bluff Inn and at Clarks Landing/Curtis Grove. In 1917 the club constructed a 9-hole course on the old Cook Tract. The Cook Homestead was used as a clubhouse until the organization was dissolved in the early 1930s. On the green in 1925 are, from left to right: Laura Reed, Harry Reed, and Nina Backes.

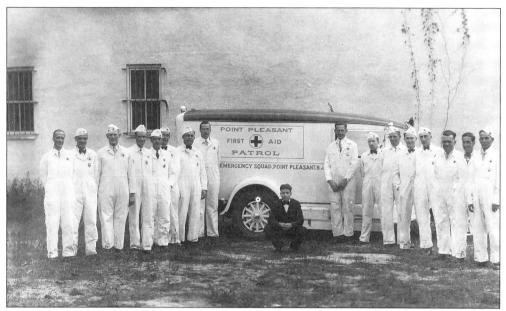

The Point Pleasant First Aid Squad was organized in 1929 and its charter members were, from left to right: Bill Watkins, Fred Hurley, Arthur Johnson, Lee Downey, Morton Gottlieb, Bill Borden, Larry Goble, Joe Bagnall, Russ Archer, Harry Hobart, Ridgeway Lane, Joe Lunetta, Al Smith, Bill Makin, and Norman Cramer.

The squad's first ambulance was a converted Studebaker van, shown here at Point Pleasant Hospital's original entrance in 1936. Point Pleasant Hospital was founded in 1918 by Dr. Frank Denniston at 422 River Avenue in the Beach. The hospital was moved to its present site in Point Pleasant Borough in 1927. After numerous expansions and renovations the hospital today is part of the Medical Center of Ocean County.

The Point Pleasant First Aid Squad had its home in Carver's Garage on Arnold Avenue the first four years of its existence. New quarters were built on Laurel Avenue in 1933 (above) with Borough Hall occupying the second floor. The squad originally served Point Pleasant, Brick Township, and Bay Head south to Seaside. Point Pleasant Borough formed its own first aid squad in 1968.

The Point Pleasant Beach Hospital (not associated with Point Pleasant Hospital) at Richmond and Forman Avenues in 1948. This hospital was run by Dr. Harry Ivory and is today the Point Pleasant Beach Nursing Home (it was the original site of the Forman Homestead, see page 17).

Point Pleasant Beach Fire Company No. 2 was formed in 1907 and was originally based at Bay and Laurel Avenues. Members c. 1915 were, from left to right: Lou Callaghan, Ed Davis, Sam Lane, Sam Chafey, Father Bohart, Dr. Grube, Albert Fleming (with ax), Leon Germain, Dr. Tindell, Clarence Worth, Martin Hyers, John Callaghan (with nozzle), Walter Makin, Clarence Lovell, Harry Pearce, unknown, Walter Alberti (helmet and nozzle), Joseph Lynch, Joe Vetrini, Joe McIlhenny, and John Moore.

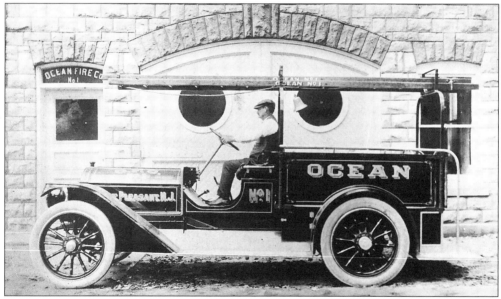

Ocean Fire Company No. 1 was organized in 1885 and became the first such company in Ocean County. Its first permanent headquarters was located on Cramer Avenue. Some early fire fighting equipment included two dozen buckets and a $400 hook and ladder truck which was housed in a rented building on Ocean Road. In 1899 the company built John Arnold Hall as its headquarters (see page 35). A new firehouse on River Avenue was dedicated in 1915 (shown above). Ocean Fire Company No. 1 remained in this building until 1964 when it moved to its present location on Arnold Avenue.

The first Point Pleasant Borough Hall at the corner of Arnold Avenue and Ocean Road in 1926. The first floor housed stores and Point Pleasant Fire Company No. 1, organized in 1920. Point Pleasant Fire Company No. 2 was formed in 1954. This municipal building was torn down in the mid-1960s and today the site is the home of a Dunkin Donuts. The present municipal building is located on Bridge Avenue.

The Point Pleasant Beach Municipal Building as it appeared in 1948 when it served as the water plant. The original Point Pleasant Beach water plant was located to the rear of the trolley power house with the water tank on the roof, and it served the community until 1926. The 212,000-gallon standpipe was removed in the late 1960s.

The Point Pleasant Traction Company power house on Atlantic Avenue next to the railroad tracks *c*. 1912. Early electric automobiles could also pull up and plug in. The power house provided electricity to Point Pleasant and surrounding towns from 1896 to 1914 and still exists today as a JCP&L substation. The Point Pleasant Electric Light and Power Company also had their own crew (above) for maintaining the system.

In the days of gravel roads, street sprinklers were often used to help keep down the dust kicked up by the wind and passing automobiles. This four-ton Mack truck was purchased for $6,600 in 1920 and is shown doing its job in 1923.

The Point Pleasant Borough Water Works was built in 1936 on Florence Avenue (now Albert E. Clifton Avenue), ending the Boro's dependence on water supplied by Point Pleasant Beach. The pump house contained the latest in water plant technology.

Point Pleasant's first elevated water tank and pumping station on Florence Avenue in 1936. The municipal garage is in the distance.

During the 1920s, residents of Point Pleasant enjoyed the protection of the New Jersey State Police which was headquartered on Cramer Avenue. After a brief absence, the force returned in 1929 and was located over Carver's Garage. The Point Pleasant Station was closed for good in 1932 and consolidated with the Farmingdale Station. Here, a state police motorcycle patrol is shown on East Avenue with Bay Head patrolman George Smythe.

Writing a parking ticket on Bay Avenue in July 1948. The modern Point Pleasant Beach Police Department was formed in 1928 with Ridgeway T. Lane appointed its first police chief. The department moved into Borough Hall in 1929 and has since grown into a very effective organization. Point Pleasant Borough's Police Department was created in 1930. Prior to the establishment of these departments, both municipalities were served by town marshals.

The St. Vincent Home for Orphans was opened in 1888 as a seashore summer home for Philadelphia-area children. These children were very much a part of the community each summer, participating in social functions and performing with their own choir at the hotels. The home was located on Richmond Avenue between New Jersey and Atlantic Avenues and was later renamed St. Joseph Home. The building was torn down in sections during the 1950s with the chapel remaining today as the home of the Durand Masonic Lodge.

One of Point Pleasant's many community organizations, Atlantic Council 154 of the Junior Order of United American Mechanics, in 1911. Shown here are, from left to right: (first row) Abe Lawrence, Bill Sutphen, Thomas Tilton, Fred Pearce, Carl Hankins, Mr. Murphy, Bob Pearce, unknown, Hank VanNote, and Delores Pearce; (back row) Riley VanNote, Ezra Hankins, Ed Burdge, unknown, unknown, Floyd Osborn, unknown, Fred Lee, Russell Matthews, Frank Sculthorpe, Randolph Hulse, Ray Alberti, and Barzilla Asay.

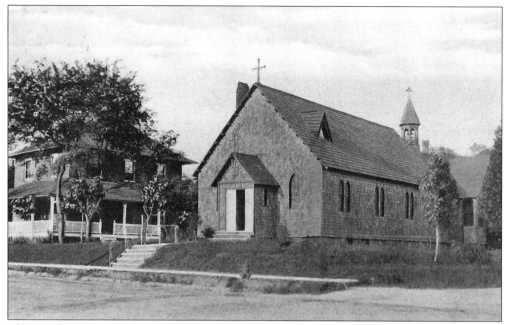

The St. Mary's Episcopal Church at Bay and Atlantic Avenues in 1910. Church services began on August 31, 1873, and by July 4, 1880, a church building was opened on land donated by John Arnold at the northwest corner of White Lawn Cemetery. The church was moved to its present site in 1889 and still remains today as Point Pleasant Beach's oldest church.

The Harvey Memorial Church on Arnold Avenue in 1951. Originally named the First Methodist Episcopal Church of Point Pleasant, the church society was formed on February 19, 1853, with the original church standing on the north side of Lakewood Road just west of the present canal. The present church was completed in 1873 and was later renamed after long-time church supporter J.H. Harvey.

The Point Pleasant Presbyterian Church at Bay and Forman Avenues in 1907. The Presbyterian Society grew out of a summer Sunday school held for neighborhood children by Dr. Charles Knox of Bloomfield. Incorporation followed on July 31, 1882, and the present church building was built the following year.

The First Baptist Church of Point Pleasant Beach was organized in 1888 and the present church was built that year on McLean Avenue, the property having been donated by William Curtis. The church building was moved one lot east to its present corner location in 1894 and was remodeled and enlarged in 1926. The Reverend William H. Mayo was the first resident clergyman.

The First Church of Christ, Scientist had a modest beginning in 1929, holding services in several locations before purchasing the old Mary Arnold home at 407 River Avenue (above). Church services were held on the first floor with Sunday school classes on the second floor. In 1956 the church had a pre-fabricated church built at 301 River Avenue.

The Central United Methodist Church on Arnold Avenue was an outgrowth of the Harvey Memorial Church, with the new congregation organizing in 1919. The church building, shown here in 1947, was completed in 1922 and has changed little in appearance, except for the addition of a spire in 1969.

St. Peter's Roman Catholic Church at Forman and St. Louis Avenues in 1910. The parish was started by Reverend Peter Jachetti in 1881, when he missed the train to Manchester (his intended destination) and ended up in Point Pleasant Beach. The original church was built the following year on Richmond Avenue between Washington and Newark Avenues. This church burned in 1901 and the present church, designed by Henry Dagit of Philadelphia, was dedicated on July 27, 1902. The marble sanctuary was finished in 1919.

St. Peter's Parochial School, the first in Ocean County, opened its doors in September 1924. The original school on Atlantic Avenue today serves as the parish hall. A new school was completed in September 1957 with sixteen classrooms and a cafeteria. An auditorium and gymnasium were added in 1962.

The first public school in Point Pleasant was built in 1867 on Arnold Avenue opposite Lincoln Avenue. A second one-room school was built the following year south of Lakewood Road at the present canal and was known as Pine Grove Academy. This school burned in 1900 and the first Ocean Road School (shown above) was erected in 1901, housing grades one through eight.

A class portrait at the Ocean Road School c. 1903. This school burned to the ground in March of 1915.

After the 1915 fire, a new school was immediately built and stood for over seventy-five years before it was torn down and replaced by the present elementary school. Large additions were made to Ocean Road School in 1930 and 1950. This photograph was taken in 1926.

Before school-sponsored sporting activities were adopted, many local groups organized and played similar teams from other towns. Baseball, basketball, and football were played at several local fields around the turn of the century. This cotton-quilted 1896 football uniform shows they were a serious bunch (see page 71).

A new multi-room school was built in 1888 at Trenton and Gowdy Avenues in Point Pleasant Beach. Elementary grades were held in the first-floor classrooms, while grades seven and eight were in a room on the second floor. Next to this classroom was a large assembly room called Education Hall. In 1893 a 450-pound bell was purchased for the school's bell tower.

Point Pleasant Beach's first school featured large classrooms where several classes were taught at one time. By 1900, kindergarten through two years of high school were being taught here. The first graduation from the two-year high school program was held in Arnold Hall in 1902 when three students graduated. A four-year high school program was instituted the following year and in 1906 its first five graduates received diplomas.

Recess on the steps of the first Point Pleasant Beach school in 1899. This school was destroyed by fire in February 1908 and was replaced by the one in the photograph below.

Point Pleasant Beach's second school opened in 1909 and was typical of the county schools built at this time. The four-story brick building contained ten classrooms and an auditorium on the top floor. Fire again struck in July 1912 when this school was gutted. That September classes were held in the Backes Building (now the Antique Emporium) while the school was rebuilt minus the fourth floor. This building was torn down in 1973.

In 1922 a new high school was completed in Point Pleasant Beach (shown above), relieving the severely overcrowded conditions in the old school, which was then used as a grammar school. A second addition to the high school opened in 1937 and this school continues to serve Point Pleasant Beach, Bay Head, and Mantoloking. Point Pleasant Borough students gradually moved out of the school and into their own high school starting in 1962.

Point Pleasant Beach High School football team practicing in front of the school on Trenton Avenue in 1926. Football and baseball events were later held at Clayton Field (opposite top), while basketball was played in the gymnasium which was located in the basement beneath the high school auditorium. A 1963 addition to the school provided a larger, more modern gym.

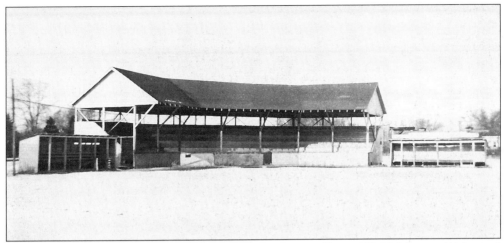

A photograph of the grandstand and baseball dugouts at Clayton Field between Richmond Avenue and the railroad in 1948. The municipal field was built in 1928 and named in memory of councilman Spencer Clayton who died that year. Activity at Clayton Field began to gradually end when the new Antrim School field opened in 1955.

In 1953 voters approved the construction of a twelve-room elementary school on Niblick Street, shown here in 1969. This was the former site of the Cook Homestead and the Point Pleasant Golf Course. The school was dedicated in 1955 as the Niblick Street School but was renamed in memory of Supervising Principal G. Harold Antrim, who died shortly after the school was completed.

The beach front excluded, Clark's Landing on the Manasquan River was the most popular entertainment spot in the history of Point Pleasant. The complex, shown in its heyday during the 1920s, was started by Roderick Clark in 1872 as a boat building and renting concern which gradually evolved into a popular boating and fishing spot on the river. Clark's son Rosia built a two-story pavilion in 1894, featuring a fabulous ice cream saloon. A large dance floor was added when the pavilion was enlarged in 1903.

Clark's Landing became known throughout the state for its many attractions, from picnicking and dances to sailboat races and crabbing. Fireworks, free movies, and a photo gallery were also popular. Over a thousand picnickers would occupy the grounds and docks on any given summer day. During the winter the rowboats went into sheds and ice sailing and skating on the Manasquan River became the main attraction.

The building on the left housed an 1896 carousel and steam organ at Clark's Landing. The entrance road is along the bottom of this 1920 photograph, while the house on the right was situated on Arnold Avenue at the bend. In the background is the old golf links and ball field followed by the first houses built on Lincoln Avenue. Clark's Landing was sold out of the family in the mid-1920s and gradually evolved into a marina, which remains today.

Civil War Veteran Roderick A. Clark came to Point Pleasant with his parents in 1848 and took up boat building with his father, John. Clark enlisted in the war in 1862 and fought in many important battles before losing his lower left leg to infection from a gunshot wound. He came back to Point Pleasant in 1865, later serving as a chosen freeholder and on the state assembly. Roderick Clark died in 1929 at the age of 86.

Ye Olde Tyme Songs

For the

"Community Sing"

POINT PLEASANT

::: N e w J e r s e y :::

Direction of Mr. Jay Wellington

A "GET-TO-GETHER" MOVEMENT TO GIVE *The* WORLD *The* GREATEST EXPRESSION OF *The* UNSELFISH, NEIGHBORLY, PROGRESSIVE SPIRIT OF *The* COAST TOWN BEAUTIFUL.

"That Ye May Love One Another"

EXECUTIVE STAFF

FINIANCE COMMMITTEE

Mr. Clarence Chafey Mr. W. D. Stanford

PROGRAM COMMITTEE

Mrs. Frank Blake, *Chairman*

Mrs. Frank Dennison Mrs. Frederic Wack Mrs. Evelyn Christie

USHERS

Mr. Daniel McElhinney, *Chief Usher*

Mr. Reed Gager Mr. Earl Limroth Mr. Thomas Harper Mr. Frank Stanford

Accompanist: Mrs. A. O. S. Havens

Silver Offerings for the Benefit of Local Organizations.

A REQUEST--:-Please Return This Book of Songs to One of The Ushers.

Five
Maritime Memories

Looking south from Manasquan toward Ralph Borden's Inlet Pavilion in 1913. The Manasquan Inlet can be seen flowing through the dunes near the pavilion. The inlet closed up completely in 1926 and it was common to travel to Manasquan by going 'around' the river on the beach.

The House River and Harbor Commission gave the green light for the opening of Manasquan Inlet in January 1930 and construction began on May 19 by jetty builder Jesse Howland of Sea Bright. This is the view east in June 1930 from the center of the future inlet. Stones for the jetties were excavated from the New York Subway, then under construction, and brought down by railcars. The jetties were completed December 27.

Once the jetties were built, a dredge worked its way down the Manasquan River and removed the sand from west to east. River and ocean waters first mingled on February 10, 1931, and a permanent opening was competed in July. Such a large project continuously drew large crowds to the inlet area on both sides.

The suction dredge hard at work in the growing inlet channel in July 1931. The sand and water was pumped through large pipes to the beach in Manasquan, where it was already known an erosion problem was imminent in the coming years. The Manasquan Inlet was officially opened on August 29, 1931, and cost $600,000 to build.

Several water events were held at Manasquan Inlet during the 1930s. This 150-foot diving tower on the Squan side was part of the Manasquan Celebration in August 1939. Notice the Navy blimp in the background.

This series of photographs shows a boat-righting drill performed by the crew of the Manasquan Coast Guard Station on July 4, 1937.

At this time the Coast Guard was still stationed in Manasquan. The Point Pleasant Beach Station was under construction.

This drill was part of the July Fourth festivities at Manasquan Beach and was held just north of the inlet jetty.

With the skiff righted, the crew then rowed in to the beach. This was a routine drill of the Coast Guard Service.

Hauling the Coast Guard's skiff ashore was a big job, as shown here on Manasquan Beach in 1931. Human muscle was soon replaced by tractors for bringing the boats on the beach, an activity which itself disappeared by the late 1940s.

The Manasquan Inlet Coast Guard Station (then called Squan Beach Station) shortly before its completion in December 1937. The station was built at a cost of $42,000 and was officially dedicated with much fanfare on January 30, 1938.

Desolation surrounded the station in its first decade in Point Pleasant Beach. The boat house across Inlet Drive was completed in late 1938 and a lookout tower on the beach was added about 1942.

Until 1875, the only way to cross the Manasquan River was to travel over the Allen Osborn bridge (near the present Route 70 bridge). On June 5, 1875, the first bridge between Point Pleasant and Union Landing was opened. While benefiting both sides of the river, the wooden bridge, shown here in 1896, was in constant need of repair and was eventually condemned in 1895, and remained open only to pedestrians and bicycles.

In 1897 a new iron bridge (above) was built across the Manasquan River, replacing the wooden structure. This $40,000 bridge featured a 20-foot wide roadway and 5-foot walk. It was 2,000 feet long with a 125-foot swing draw. Although the pride of both counties, the iron superstructure soon began to rot in the marine air, and by 1920 the bridge was in danger of collapsing.

Another bridge that spanned the Manasquan River carried the railroad. This wood-pile trestle was built in 1880 and featured a hand-operated swing draw. Half of this trestle was filled with soil and rock in 1906 and a new steel and concrete draw was completed in 1912 (shown above). The timber trestle itself was replaced by the present bridge in 1917.

Work on the third Manasquan River bridge between Point Pleasant Beach and Brielle began in December 1921 and wasn't completed until April 1925. It was built just west of the iron bridge, and the southern half consisted of fill taken from the Manasquan-Bay Head Canal excavations. The bridge, shown in 1941, had a serious flaw in that it had only 10 feet of clearance for marine traffic. Constant bridge openings made miles of auto backups commonplace.

On August 20, 1946, near disaster struck when the Manasquan River bridge collapsed. Fortunately there were no cars on the two northernmost spans when they fell due to severe erosion at the base of the support caisson. The bridge was closed to traffic for months before a temporary span was placed over the collapsed section.

Plans were drawn for a new four-lane bridge in 1946. Two years of debate followed between the neighboring towns and the state on the location of the bridge and its approaches. Construction of the new bridge got under way in 1949.

The present Route 35 bridge rises from the Manasquan River in May 1950. Much of the fill from the old bridge was removed as the main river channel was relocated 200 feet south. Route 35 was completely rebuilt from the Brielle Circle east to the bridge. In Point Pleasant Beach, Route 35 was dualized coming off the bridge in anticipation of continuing the dualization through the Borough at a future date, which is eventually what happened.

The grand opening of the new Veterans of All Wars Memorial Bridge on May 25, 1951. Guests of honor included officials from both counties, state highway officials, and New Jersey Governor Robert Meyner. Local and military bands and an antique auto parade rounded out the festivities.

The Manasquan-Bay Head Canal (now the Point Pleasant Canal) was a dream and desire of many area residents for over eighty years before construction of the canal was begun on January 4, 1916. Work was halted during the First World War in 1917 but was resumed by the LeChard Dredging Company the following year. Work progressed very slowly for the next seven years as costs escalated and state funds remained elusive.

As the canal was dug, the steam shovel placed the sand and earth along the banks. On December 15, 1925, the Delaware Dredging Company broke through at the Manasquan River with the usual gathering of state and local dignitaries. A special banquet was held at the Berkeley-Carteret Hotel in Asbury Park on January 16 to celebrate the opening.

The original Lakewood Road bridge over the canal in 1933. Lakewood Road was closed to traffic in 1923 as the canal work cut through the road and traffic was detoured to Pine Bluff Avenue. In January 1924 construction began on the bridge, which was completed in September. After sixty-two years of service the Route 88 bridge was replaced by the present vertical lift bridge.

The swing draw is open on the original Lovelandtown bridge in 1952. This bridge was built in 1929 in response to outcries from residents in Lovelandtown to the east and those in Dorsettown on the west side of the new canal, which had isolated the two neighborhoods from each other. Part of this bridge collapsed in the March storm of 1962 and a new Lovelandtown bridge was completed in 1972.

The Johnson Brothers Boat Works in 1938. Zachariah and Abraham Johnson established the works in 1922 at the Barnegat Bay entrance to the canal. The boat works excelled in the construction of Barbay skiffs and, later, custom built boats up to 65 feet in length.

In 1890 Morton Johnson started a boat yard on Barnegat Bay in Bay Head and built it into one of the most important establishments of its kind at the shore. Morton Johnson built boats for the Army and specialized in commercial lifeboats such as the one shown here in 1944.

Morton Johnson's son Hubert was destined to enter into his father's trade, and he opened his own boat yard next to his father's in 1912. Hubert Johnson was a true marine engineer, building speed runabouts and sea skiffs while maintaining a fully equipped machine shop for the repair of boat and race car engines. Hubert Johnson's work was recognized around the world. His boat works are shown here in 1942.

Wartime military vessels under construction at the Morton Johnson Boat Works in 1943.

In 1898 William K. Blodgett put in a fish pound at the foot of what is now Elizabeth Avenue, and he became one of the first of many successful pound fishermen in Ocean County. Blodgett's pound eventually employed sixteen men and shipped fresh fish as far as eastern Pennsylvania. Blodgett's pound closed by the mid-1910s. When the *Lizzie H. Brayton* sank in 1904, Blodgett purchased the wreck and used the still standing mast as an anchor pole for his fleet of pound boats (above).

Hauling in the catch at the Point Pleasant Fishery pound off Sea Girt in June 1947. By this time the beach-based pound fisheries were closing as commercial fishing moved farther offshore. Carlson's Point Pleasant Fishery and the Manasquan River Fishery continued to operate pounds off Point Pleasant Beach through the 1950s.

The fish pounds were all based on one proven design. Starting about 1/2 mile offshore and heading seaward was the weir, a wall of nets and rope that guided the fish into the forbay. The forbay kept the fish from swimming back out to sea and guided them into the funnel and pocket. The pocket had sides and a bottom made of netting, which would be raised with the daily catch, sometimes approaching 5,000 pounds. The pound nets were hung on 70- to 80-foot hickory poles.

The pound nets were in constant need of attention and repairs. Crews from the Seashore Fish Company are shown here mending their nets in the open land off Channel Drive in 1942. The Seashore Fish Company was located on Wills Hole Thoroughfare midway between Baltimore and Chicago Avenues.

A pound crew takes a break while unloading the catch at Carlson's dock in May 1944. All of the common local species of fish were caught in the pounds, including the occasional shark, tuna, and sea turtle. Once the fish were brought to the dock, they were packed into baskets and unloaded, all by hand.

Once on the dock, the crews expertly cleaned and filleted the fish and packed them in ice. The fish were then crated and shipped by truck to the various seafood outlets in the metropolitan areas. Point Pleasant Fishery, shown here in 1942, was started in 1936 by Axel Carlson who had earlier worked the Seaside Fisheries. His two sons, Walter and Axel "Junie" Carlson Jr. were also involved with the business and eventually took it over.

Every now and then, a monster of a fish would be brought in on the pound boats and cause quite a stir, such as this giant tuna did at Carlson's in 1944.

Showing off a couple of local lobsters at Carlson's dock are, from left to right: Walter "Buddy" and Axel Carlson Sr., Lucien D. Truhill, Stanley J. Blair, Leon Germain, Point Pleasant Mayor Ralph A. Carlson, Governor Robert B. Meyner, and Robert Kronowitt. The event was the Greater Point Pleasant Fishing Derby in July 1956.

Forsberg's Boat Works, Inc.

Repaired — CUSTOM BUILT BOATS — Stored

MARINE SUPPLIES   PAINTS

1692 West End Drive, Point Pleasant, N. J.

TWinbrook 2-4246

PURCHASE AGREEMENT

I hereby agree to purchase ....

....

....

with accessories as follows: ....

....

....

For the sum of $........................

Cost of Access. $........................

Total $........................

to be paid as follows:
25% upon signing this agreement; 25% upon completion of hull; 25% upon installation of motor; 25% or balance on de-

livery at shipyard on or about ....

Until the entire purchase price is paid, the Customer agrees:

    a. That the boat will not be removed from the shipyard and that the Customer will be responsible for any loss by reason of theft, fire, or casualty.

    b. Title to the boat shall not pass to the Customer and the Company may repossess the article immediately upon default.

Dated the .... day of ...., 19.......

Signed by ....

Customer

....

Witness

Home Address: ....

Summer Address: ....

Phone: ....

All orders subject to acceptance by Company.

Accepted

FORSBERG'S BOAT WORKS, Inc.

....

Forsberg's Boat Works was started in 1945 on the Beaver Dam Creek by Karl Forsberg and his wife Margaret. The business still prospers today.

Six

Let's Visit
the Boardwalk

A typical outing at the beach . . . 1890s style. This group of Cook Homestead guests are enjoying a day at the inlet in 1898.

The first pavilion at the Manasquan Inlet was put up by William Reed and Frank Chamberlain in 1896, serving hot coffee, sandwiches, homemade pies, and ice cream. The pavilion and bath houses were very popular with the homestead guests as well as the many fishermen who frequented the inlet.

The new owners of the Cook Farm built a new Inlet Pavilion in 1903. The 40- by 50-foot building contained a restaurant on the ground floor and an open sitting area above that was later enclosed. Other buildings nearby included a dance hall and an outdoor merry-go-round. Steam launches were run daily between the Inlet Pavilion and Clark's Landing.

With the Manasquan Inlet as a backdrop, a young crowd of beachgoers mug for the camera in 1899, woolen bathing suits and all.

Down the beach at the Beacon-By-The-Sea Hotel stood this bathing pavilion which somewhat resembled a schoolhouse. This pavilion dated back to the 1870s and was operated by the hotel for its guests. A portable boardwalk was added by the time this photograph was taken in 1906. Playing in the sand from left to right are: Maude Holman, Alvin Holman, and Helen Gilbert.

Our beach has also been the scene of many a shipwreck. In the evening of February 12, 1900, the four-masted ship *County of Edinburgh* came ashore near the foot of Arnold Avenue. On its way to New York from Cape Town, South Africa, the Scottish vessel found itself caught in westerly currents and came ashore in moderate seas.

The *County of Edinburgh* remained on the bar for thirteen days before it was refloated and towed off. Other notable wrecks off the beaches of Point Pleasant include the *Alabama* in February 1846, the Hazard and Memento in 1862, the Civita Carrara in 1888, the Lizzie Brayton in 1904, and the George S. Phillips in 1905.

The coastal storms of April 1929 were among the most damaging ever to strike Point Pleasant Beach. The combination of narrow beaches, heavy erosion, and back-to-back nor'easters created havoc and heavy property damage along the beach front. During the second storm on April 16 the east wing of the Leighton Hotel collapsed in ruins. James Chafey's boardwalk pharmacy (foreground) also fell victim to the raging seas.

The inlet section suffered the most damage during these storms with thirteen bungalows destroyed and most of the boardwalk lost or damaged. During the gale every attempt was made to save the bungalow colony from the hungry Atlantic, which at times washed across Ocean Avenue and into Lake Louise. Many homeowners frantically moved their bungalows away from the beach or had long piling pumped in during and between the two storms.

The boardwalk south of Central Avenue in June 1930. The beach was in bad shape with the undertow dangerously close to the boardwalk. The four bungalows on the left were later replaced by Frank's Arcade. The Boardwalk Lunch and Grill later became the Ripe Tide Bar and today is Major's. With the completion of the Manasquan Inlet jetties in 1931, the beach soon made a rapid recovery.

The Point Pleasant Fishing Club pier during a nor'easter in March 1931. The fishing club first built a 300-foot pier in 1918, only to have it wash away the following summer. A new sturdier pier 800 feet in length was quickly built by the club, which had grown to become the largest fishing club on the East Coast with over 950 members. This new pier featured a bait and tackle shop on the seaward end and the Sea Breeze Restaurant near the boardwalk.

The beach front has also felt its share of dreaded hurricanes, as seen here at Forman Avenue in 1938. The September 1938 hurricane took out most of the boardwalk between Arnold Avenue and the Beacon Hotel. The hurricane of 1944 inflicted even more widespread damage throughout the area. Other notable hurricanes to strike the Point Pleasant area included several during the mid-1950s, Hurricane Belle in 1976, and Gloria in 1985.

A Navy blimp out of Lakehurst keeps a watchful eye on the coastal waters off Point Pleasant Beach in June 1942. The threat of submarine attacks during World War II made constant surveillance necessary from land and air. Blackout curtains were erected along the boardwalk amusement areas to hide the shoreline lights (which could be used as a target by the Nazis) and also to prevent the lights from silhouetting any seaward vessels for the U-boats.

In 1917 the north end of the boardwalk was at the Active Club just north of Central Avenue. Beyond this point planks were placed between the dunes to the Inlet Pavilion. The Active Club was founded in 1890 by a group of Newark baseball players who called themselves the "Actives." Looking for a summer home, they came to Point Pleasant Beach in 1909 and purchased an oceanfront home from the Cooke estate. Club members and their families continued to summer at the boardwalk clubhouse into the early 1960s.

The fishing pier and foot of Arnold Avenue in 1927. The Wuest Casino (left) was built in 1893 and later became the home to the first boardwalk carousel. This building survived eighty years before it was destroyed in the big boardwalk fire in April 1975.

The boardwalk and beach at Atlantic Avenue in 1919. The first boardwalk was built in this section in the mid-1880s. Being portable, this narrow walkway was removed off its piling and stored during the winter months. The Borough began to lease this boardwalk and the right-of-way in 1896, extending it north to Arnold Avenue in 1901. In 1915 a new permanent boardwalk was built between Central and Philadelphia Avenues and was later extended to the Manasquan Inlet and Beacon Hotel, a distance of almost 1 1/2 miles.

The original Resort House Bathing Pavilion, shown here c. 1920, was built in 1884 as a beach front destination for the hotel's horse trolley. Everett E. Johnson purchased the pavilion from the Murphy Estate in 1913 and thereafter it was known as Johnson's. In the background is Joseph Risden's Pavilion, formerly known as the "Pastimes." Risden's Casino became a boardwalk institution for over fifty years, and eventually became known as the Hoffman House Night Club.

In January 1926 Charles H. Jenkinson of Asbury Park purchased the beach front at the foot of Parkway. Two years later he built Jenkinson's Pavilion and pool. The $100,000 complex officially opened July 7, 1928, and featured the largest outdoor salt water pool between Asbury Park and Atlantic City. The open air pavilion housed several concessions with a bandstand in the center. A biplane can be seen buzzing the fishing pier and Jenkinson's Pavilion in the opening season of a boardwalk tradition in Point Pleasant Beach.

After a very successful first year, Jenkinson's Pavilion was enlarged and enclosed in 1929. The pavilion now featured a new dance hall complete with a ten-piece orchestra and a new soda fountain. For the next fifteen years the big band craze swept the pavilion's 2,000-square-foot dance floor with the likes of Johnny Johnson and Sammy Kaye, and was frequently broadcast live on national radio. The original pavilion met a fiery fate in 1989 and has since been rebuilt.

Jenkinson's salt water pool in its opening year, 1928. The concrete pool was constantly replenished with filtered sea water that was drawn through pipes run under the pavilion and into the Atlantic.

One of many strictly enforced rules at Jenkinson's pool was to always shower off the beach sand before entering the pool. The showers, bath houses, and pool all disappeared in 1980 as maintenance of the pool was becoming prohibitive and the need for more parking prevailed.

An unusual view of the beach and boardwalk in 1927 from near Niblick Street. The comfort station is at the foot of Parkway, followed by the fishing pier and the Sea Breeze Restaurant. One year later Jenkinson's was built, hiding this wide-open view of the beach front in Point Pleasant Beach.

The southern end of town became popular with bathers when the Beacon Baths opened in the mid-1930s. This photograph was taken in August 1936 when one could still walk the entire beach front on the boardwalk. A two-story concession and apartment was added in 1938, and these structures still serve the patrons of Beacon Beach.

The boardwalk at Jenkinson's Pavilion in July 1950. Many new boardwalk attractions appeared during the 1950s, geared mostly toward the younger crowd. These included kiddy rides at Holiday Play land and Jenkinson's Inlet Pavilion (remember the live monkeys?), Jenkinson's beach train, Frank's Arcade, and Herman's Amusements.

The original Martell's Playhouse and Sea Breeze Restaurant in September 1950. These buildings were built by Caroline Hutchinson in 1939 and later sold to Fred Martell. The Sea Breeze Restaurant was first located on the fishing pier and later purchased by Thomas Hall in 1927. The restaurant was moved into a new addition to Martell's around 1950. Martell's bar and dance floor featured live entertainment during the 1950s and 60s, giving early exposure to the Four Seasons and other New Jersey-based pop groups.

125

Point Pleasant Beach seen from the south in 1958.

The Beacon-By-The-Sea and still largely undeveloped land around Lake of the Lillies in May 1946.

126

Point Pleasant Beach and Point Pleasant from the north in 1948.

Martell's and Jenkinson's seen from above in May 1946. Notice the still undeveloped land west of Lake Louise.